contents

Please note that Australian cup and spoon measurements are metric.
A conversion chart appears on page 62.

Slow cooked
soups · casseroles · roasts

Advantages of slow-cooking

Great taste Slow-cooked food is tender, moist and succulent – these are the common qualities of all slow-cooked dishes, whether it's a casserole, a curry or a roast.

Time-saving Another thing they all have in common is that once they've had their initial preparation, most slow-cooked food can be left alone to bubble away while you get on with other things.

Cheap Slow-cooked casseroles, curries and stews can (and should) be made with cheap cuts of meat. They have more fat marbled through them, which makes them perfect for long, slow cooking. Lean meat would simply become dry. This means, of course, that you save money on slow-cooked dishes – you don't use a huge amount of energy either, even though you're cooking for such a long time, because you have your oven or stove top turned to low.

No-cook nights When slow-cooking soups, casseroles, curries and other dishes that benefit from being eaten the next day, make at least double the quantity you need for one meal and freeze the rest in serving-sized batches. Defrost in the fridge and heat in the microwave or in a pan over low heat, then all you have to do is cook some rice or a few vegetables and you have a delicious, nourishing and lovingly prepared family dinner – and the bliss of an almost no-cook night.

Surprising roasts If you've never tasted a slow-cooked leg of lamb roasted the Greek way, you're in for a wonderful surprise. The meat falls off the bone and can be cut with a fork – it's one of the most delicious ways to cook lamb. Lamb shanks are a similar story – they're sweet, succulent and tender when cooked for several hours. Pork also benefits from slow-roasting, especially cheaper cuts such as the neck.

soups

hungarian goulash soup

2 tablespoons olive oil
40g butter
900g boneless veal shoulder,
   cut into 2cm pieces
2 medium brown onions
   (300g), chopped finely
1 tablespoon tomato paste
1 tablespoon plain flour
1 tablespoon sweet paprika
2 teaspoons caraway seeds
½ teaspoon cayenne pepper
2 cloves garlic, crushed
2 cups (500ml) water
1.5 litres (6 cups) beef stock
400g can diced tomatoes
1 large red capsicum (350g),
   chopped coarsely
1 medium potato (200g),
   chopped coarsely
spätzle
1 cup (150g) plain flour
2 eggs, beaten lightly
¼ cup (60ml) water
½ teaspoon cracked
   black pepper

1   Heat half the oil and half the butter in large saucepan; cook veal, in batches, until browned.
2   Heat remaining oil and butter in same pan; cook onion, stirring, about 5 minutes or until onion is slightly caramelised.
3   Add paste, flour, paprika, seeds, cayenne and garlic; cook, stirring, 2 minutes. Return veal to pan with the water, stock and undrained tomatoes; bring to the boil. Simmer, uncovered, 1½ hours. Add capsicum and potato; simmer about 10 minutes or until potato is tender.
4   Meanwhile, make spätzle.
5   Serve bowls of soup topped with spätzle.
spätzle   Sift flour into small bowl, make well in centre. Gradually add combined egg and the water, stirring, until batter is smooth; stir in pepper. Pour batter into metal colander set over large saucepan of boiling water; using a wooden spoon, push batter through holes of colander. Bring water back to the boil; boil, uncovered, about 2 minutes or until spätzle float to the surface. Use a slotted spoon to remove spätzle; drain before adding to soup.

prep & cook time 2 hours 25 minutes
serves 4
nutritional count per serving 27.3g total fat
(9.5g saturated fat); 3022kJ (723 cal);
48g carbohydrate; 68.8g protein; 5.8g fibre
note Recipe is not suitable to freeze.

beef and barley soup

1 tablespoon olive oil
500g gravy beef, trimmed, cut into 2cm pieces
2 cloves garlic, crushed
2 medium brown onions (300g), chopped finely
¾ cup (150g) pearl barley
3 cups (750ml) beef stock
1.5 litres (6 cups) water
1 bay leaf
1 sprig fresh rosemary
1 sprig fresh thyme
2 medium potatoes (400g), cut into 1cm pieces
2 medium carrots (240g), cut into 1cm pieces
2 medium zucchini (240g), cut into 1cm pieces
2 medium yellow patty-pan squash (60g), cut into 1cm pieces
100g swiss brown mushrooms, chopped coarsely
½ cup finely chopped fresh flat-leaf parsley

1 Heat half the oil in large saucepan; cook beef, in batches, until
browned all over.
2 Heat remaining oil in same pan; cook garlic and onion, stirring, until
onion softens. Return beef to pan with barley, stock, the water, bay leaf,
rosemary and thyme; bring to the boil. Reduce heat; simmer, covered,
about 1 hour or until beef and barley are tender, skimming fat occasionally.
3 Add potato, carrot, zucchini, squash and mushrooms to soup; simmer,
covered, about 25 minutes or until vegetables are softened. Remove
and discard bay leaf, rosemary and thyme.
4 Serve bowls of soup sprinkled with parsley.

prep & cook time 2 hours 15 minutes **serves** 6
nutritional count per serving 8.8g total fat (2.6g saturated fat);
1350kJ (323 cal); 30g carbohydrate; 26.9g protein; 7.8g fibre
note Recipe is suitable to freeze for up to three months.

mexican bean and shredded pork soup

2 litres (8 cups) water
2 litres (8 cups) chicken stock
1 large carrot (180g), chopped
    coarsely
1 stalk celery (150g), trimmed,
    chopped coarsely
5 cloves garlic, unpeeled,
    bruised
6 black peppercorns
3 sprigs fresh oregano
1 bay leaf
1kg piece pork neck
1 tablespoon olive oil
1 large red onion (300g),
    chopped coarsely
1 medium red capsicum (200g),
    chopped coarsely
1 medium yellow capsicum
    (200g), chopped coarsely
2 fresh long red chillies,
    sliced thinly
2 cloves garlic, crushed
800g can chopped tomatoes
1 teaspoon ground cumin
2 tablespoons coarsely
    chopped fresh oregano
420g can kidney beans,
    rinsed, drained

1 Place the water and stock in large saucepan with carrot, celery, bruised garlic, peppercorns, oregano sprigs, bay leaf and pork; bring to the boil. Reduce heat; simmer, covered, 1 hour. Uncover; simmer 1 hour.

2 Transfer pork to medium bowl; using two forks, shred pork coarsely. Strain broth through muslin-lined sieve or colander into large heatproof bowl; discard solids.

3 Heat oil in same cleaned pan; cook onion, capsicums, chilli and crushed garlic, stirring, until vegetables soften. Return pork and broth to pan with undrained tomatoes, cumin and the chopped oregano; bring to the boil. Reduce heat; simmer, covered, 15 minutes. Add beans; simmer, covered, until soup is heated through.

prep & cook time 3 hours **serves** 6
nutritional count per serving 7.4g total fat (1.6g saturated fat); 1490kJ (356 cal); 20.8g carbohydrate; 46.5g protein; 9.1g fibre
note Recipe is not suitable to freeze.

lamb and white bean soup

1 cup (200g) dried
   cannellini beans
2 medium red capsicums
   (400g), quartered, seeds
   and membranes removed
1 tablespoon olive oil
1.5kg french-trimmed
   lamb shanks
1 large brown onion (200g),
   chopped coarsely
2 cloves garlic, quartered
2 medium carrots (240g),
   chopped coarsely
2 stalks celery (300g),
   trimmed, chopped coarsely
2 tablespoons tomato paste
1 cup (250ml) dry red wine
3 litres (12 cups) water
80g baby spinach leaves

1 Place beans in medium bowl, cover with water; stand overnight, drain. Rinse under cold water; drain.
2 Roast capsicum under hot grill, skin-side up, until skin blisters and blackens. Cover capsicum with plastic or paper for 5 minutes; peel away skin, chop capsicum finely.
3 Heat oil in large saucepan; cook lamb, in batches, until browned. Cook onion and garlic, stirring, until onion softens. Add carrot and celery; cook 2 minutes. Add paste and wine; bring to the boil then simmer 5 minutes.
4 Return lamb to pan with the water; bring to the boil. Simmer, uncovered, 2 hours, skimming fat from surface occasionally.
5 Place beans in medium saucepan of boiling water; return to the boil. Reduce heat; simmer, uncovered, about 30 minutes or until beans are almost tender. Drain.
6 Remove lamb from pan. Strain broth through muslin-lined sieve into large heatproof bowl; discard solids. When lamb is cool enough to handle, remove meat from shanks; shred coarsely. Discard bones.
7 Return broth to same cleaned pan with capsicum, beans and lamb; bring to the boil. Reduce heat; simmer, uncovered, 5 minutes. Remove from heat; stir in spinach.

note Recipe, without the spinach, is suitable to freeze for up to three months. Stir in spinach after reheating.

prep & cook time 4 hours (plus standing)
serves 4
nutritional count per serving 1.8g total fat (0.7g saturated fat); 171kJ (41 cal); 1.4g carbohydrate; 3.8g protein; 0.7g fibre

soups

harira [moroccan lamb soup]

1 cup (200g) dried chickpeas
20g butter
2 medium brown onions
 (300g), chopped finely
2 stalks celery (300g),
 trimmed, chopped finely
2 cloves garlic, crushed
4cm piece fresh ginger (20g),
 grated
1 teaspoon ground cinnamon
½ teaspoon ground
 black pepper
pinch saffron threads
500g diced lamb
3 large tomatoes (660g),
 seeded, chopped coarsely
2 litres (8 cups) hot water
½ cup (100g) brown lentils
2 tablespoons plain flour
½ cup (100g) white
 long-grain rice
½ cup firmly packed fresh
 coriander leaves
2 tablespoons lemon juice

1 Place chickpeas in medium bowl, cover with cold water; stand overnight, drain. Rinse under cold water; drain.
2 Melt butter in large saucepan; cook onion, celery and garlic, stirring, until onion softens. Add ginger, cinnamon, pepper and saffron; cook, stirring, until fragrant. Add lamb; cook, stirring, about 5 minutes or until lamb is browned. Add chickpeas and tomato; cook, stirring, about 5 minutes or until tomato softens.
3 Stir the hot water into soup mixture; bring to the boil. Simmer, covered, 45 minutes. Add lentils; simmer, covered, 1 hour.
4 Blend flour with ½ cup of slightly cooled broth in a small bowl; return to pan with rice. Cook, stirring, until soup comes to the boil and thickens slightly and rice is tender. Remove from heat; stir in coriander and juice.

prep & cook time 2 hours 40 minutes (plus standing) serves 8
nutritional count per serving 8.6g total fat (4g saturated fat); 1095kJ (262 cal); 23.6g carbohydrate; 20.1g protein; 4.8g fibre
note Recipe is suitable to freeze for up to three months.

minestrone

1 cup (200g) dried borlotti beans
1 tablespoon olive oil
1 medium brown onion (150g), chopped coarsely
1 clove garlic, crushed
¼ cup (70g) tomato paste
1.5 litres (6 cups) water
2 cups (500ml) vegetable stock
700g bottled tomato pasta sauce
1 stalk celery (150g), trimmed, chopped finely
1 medium carrot (120g), chopped finely
1 medium zucchini (120g), chopped finely
80g green beans, trimmed, chopped finely
¾ cup (135g) macaroni pasta
⅓ cup coarsely chopped fresh basil

1 Place borlotti beans in medium bowl, cover with cold water; stand overnight, drain. Rinse under cold water; drain.
2 Heat oil in large saucepan; cook onion and garlic, stirring, until onion softens. Add paste; cook, stirring, 2 minutes. Add borlotti beans to pan with the water, stock and pasta sauce; bring to the boil. Reduce heat; simmer, uncovered, about 1 hour or until beans are tender.
3 Add celery; simmer, uncovered, 10 minutes. Add carrot, zucchini and green beans; simmer, uncovered, about 20 minutes or until carrot is tender. Add pasta; simmer until pasta is tender.
4 Serve bowls of soup sprinkled with basil.

prep & cook time 2 hours (plus standing) **serves** 6
nutritional count per serving 5.5g total fat (1g saturated fat); 1095kJ (262 cal); 39.9g carbohydrate; 9.4g protein; 6.5g fibre
tips Recipe, without the basil, is suitable to freeze for up to 3 months. Sprinkle over basil after reheating soup. If you don't have any dried beans, you can add a can of rinsed, drained beans of your choice at the end of step 3 and stir until heated through; reduce the cooking time by 1 hour in step 2.

pea and ham soup with risoni

2 teaspoons olive oil
1 medium brown onion (150g), chopped coarsely
2 teaspoons ground cumin
2.5 litres (10 cups) water
2 stalks celery (300g), trimmed, chopped coarsely
2 dried bay leaves
1.5kg ham bone
1 cup (220g) risoni pasta
2 cups (240g) frozen peas
2 tablespoons finely chopped fresh mint

1   Heat oil in large saucepan; cook onion, stirring, until softened. Add cumin; cook, stirring, until fragrant. Stir in the water, celery, bay leaves and ham bone; bring to the boil. Reduce heat; simmer, covered, 1 hour, skimming fat from surface occasionally.
2   Remove bone; when cool enough to handle, cut ham from bone, discard any skin, fat and bone. Shred ham finely.
3   Return soup to the boil; stir in ham, pasta and peas. Cook, uncovered, about 5 minutes or until pasta is tender. Sprinkle soup with mint.

prep & cook time 1 hour 30 minutes **serves** 6
nutritional count per serving 3g total fat (0.6g saturated fat); 811kJ (194 cal); 30g carbohydrate; 9g protein; 4.6g fibre
note Recipe, without the mint, is suitable to freeze for up to three months. Sprinkle over mint after reheating soup.

on the stove top

irish lamb and barley stew

2 tablespoons olive oil

1kg diced lamb shoulder

1 large brown onion (200g),
   chopped coarsely

2 medium carrots (240g),
   chopped coarsely

2 stalks celery (300g),
   trimmed, chopped coarsely

2 cloves garlic, crushed

1 litre (4 cups) chicken stock

2 cups (500ml) water

1 cup (200g) pearl barley

4 sprigs fresh thyme

3 medium potatoes (600g),
   chopped coarsely

2 cups (160g) finely shredded
   cabbage

⅓ cup finely chopped fresh
   flat-leaf parsley

1 Heat half the oil in large saucepan; cook lamb, in batches, until browned.

2 Heat remaining oil in same pan; cook onion, carrot, celery and garlic, stirring, until vegetables soften. Return lamb to pan with stock, the water, barley and thyme; bring to the boil. Reduce heat; simmer, covered, 1 hour, skimming fat from surface occasionally.

3 Add potato; simmer, uncovered, about 20 minutes or until potato is tender. Add cabbage; simmer, uncovered, until cabbage is just tender. Discard thyme.

4 Serve stew sprinkled with parsley.

prep & cook time 2 hours serves 6
nutritional count per serving 22.6g total fat (8.2g saturated fat); 2224kJ (532 cal); 37.4g carbohydrate; 40.4g protein; 8.6g fibre
note Recipe is suitable to freeze at the end of step 2.

provençale beef casserole

2 tablespoons olive oil
1kg gravy beef, cut into 2cm pieces
2 rindless bacon rashers (130g), chopped finely
1 medium leek (350g), sliced thinly
2 medium carrots (240g), chopped coarsely
1 stalk celery (150g), trimmed, chopped coarsely
2 cloves garlic, crushed
400g can diced tomatoes
1½ cups (375ml) beef stock
1 cup (250ml) dry red wine
2 bay leaves
4 sprigs fresh thyme
6 sprigs fresh flat-leaf parsley
2 medium zucchini (240g), sliced thickly
½ cup (60g) seeded black olives

1 Heat oil in large saucepan; cook beef, in batches, until browned.
2 Cook bacon, leek, carrot, celery and garlic in same heated pan, stirring, until leek softens.
3 Return beef to pan with undrained tomatoes, stock, wine, bay leaves, thyme and parsley; bring to the boil. Reduce heat; simmer, covered, 1 hour, stirring occasionally.
4 Add zucchini and olives; simmer, covered, about 30 minutes or until beef is tender.
5 Remove and discard bay leaves, thyme and parsley. Serve casserole with crushed kipfler potatoes, if you like.

prep & cook time 2 hours 30 minutes **serves** 4
nutritional count per serving 25.8g total fat (7.8g saturated fat); 2458kJ (588 cal); 14.1g carbohydrate; 61.4g protein; 6.4g fibre
note Recipe is suitable to freeze at the end of step 3.

beef rendang

1.5kg beef chuck steak, trimmed, cut into 3cm pieces
400ml can coconut milk
½ cup (125ml) water
10cm stick fresh lemon grass (20g), bruised
3 fresh kaffir lime leaves, torn
spice paste
2 medium red onions (340g), chopped coarsely
4 cloves garlic, chopped coarsely
5cm piece fresh ginger (25g), chopped coarsely
2 fresh long red chillies, chopped coarsely
3 teaspoons grated fresh galangal
3 teaspoons ground coriander
1½ teaspoons ground cumin
1 teaspoon ground turmeric
1 teaspoon salt

1 Make spice paste.
2 Combine spice paste in large saucepan with beef, coconut milk, the water, lemon grass and lime leaves; bring to the boil. Reduce heat; simmer, covered, stirring occasionally, about 2 hours or until mixture thickens and beef is tender.
3 Serve the rendang with steamed jasmine rice, and accompany with combined finely chopped cucumber and finely sliced fresh red chilli in rice vinegar, if you like.
spice paste Blend or process ingredients until combined.

prep & cook time 2 hours 15 minutes **serves** 6
nutritional count per serving 25.2g total fat (16.9g saturated fat); 1952kJ (467 cal); 6.1g carbohydrate; 52.9g protein; 2.5g fibre
note Recipe is not suitable to freeze. You can make the curry a day or two before you need it; keep, covered, in the refrigerator.

italian seafood stew

1 tablespoon olive oil
1 medium brown onion (150g), chopped finely
3 cloves garlic, crushed
700g bottle tomato pasta sauce
1½ cups (375ml) fish stock
½ cup (125ml) dry white wine
2 strips lemon rind
600g uncooked medium king prawns
600g firm white fish fillets
300g clams, scrubbed
12 scallops without roe (300g)
¼ cup finely shredded fresh basil
¼ cup coarsely chopped fresh flat-leaf parsley

1 Heat oil in large saucepan; cook onion and garlic, stirring, until onion softens. Add pasta sauce, stock, wine and rind; bring to the boil. Reduce heat; simmer, covered, 20 minutes.
2 Meanwhile, shell and devein prawns, leaving tails intact. Cut fish into 2cm pieces.
3 Add clams to pan; simmer, covered, 5 minutes (discard any clams that do not open). Add prawns, fish and scallops to pan; cook, covered, stirring once, about 5 minutes or until seafood just changes colour. Stir in herbs.

prep & cook time 1 hour 10 minutes **serves** 4
nutritional count per serving 9.4g total fat (2g saturated fat);
1772kJ (424 cal); 14.5g carbohydrate; 62g protein; 4.7g fibre
note Recipe is not suitable to freeze.

pork belly and chorizo stew

2 chorizo sausages (340g), sliced thinly
600g piece pork belly, rind removed, cut into 3cm pieces
1 large brown onion (200g), sliced thinly
2 cloves garlic, crushed
1 teaspoon smoked paprika
1 large red capsicum (350g), chopped coarsely
800g can chopped tomatoes
½ cup (125ml) dry red wine
½ cup (125ml) water
400g can white beans, rinsed, drained
½ cup finely chopped fresh flat-leaf parsley

1   Cook chorizo and pork, in batches, in heated large flameproof casserole dish, stirring, until browned. Add onion and garlic to dish; cook, stirring, until onion softens.
2   Return meat to dish with paprika, capsicum, undrained tomatoes, wine and the water; bring to the boil. Reduce heat; simmer, covered, 40 minutes. Add beans; simmer, uncovered, about 20 minutes or until pork is tender and sauce thickens slightly. Serve stew sprinkled with parsley.

prep & cook time 1 hour 35 minutes **serves** 4
nutritional count per serving 55g total fat (19.1g saturated fat); 3331kJ (797 cal); 26.7g carbohydrate; 47g protein; 7.9g fibre
note Recipe is not suitable to freeze.

pot roast pork with apple and sage

1.5kg piece pork neck
1 tablespoon olive oil
600g spring onions, stems trimmed to 10cm lengths
6 large sprigs fresh sage
6 large sprigs fresh thyme
1 cup (250ml) dry white wine
2 tablespoons boiling water
40g butter
3 large apples (600g), unpeeled, cored, cut into thick wedges

1   Cook pork with 2 teaspoons of the oil in heated large heavy-based saucepan, turning, until browned all over. Add onions, herbs and wine to pan; bring to the boil. Reduce heat; simmer, covered tightly, about 1½ hours or until pork is cooked, turning pork twice during cooking time. Transfer pork and onions to serving platter; cover to keep warm.
2   Strain pan juices into serving jug; discard solids. Stir the water into jug; cover to keep sauce warm.
3   Meanwhile, heat butter and remaining oil in large frying pan; cook apple, stirring, about 10 minutes or until tender and golden.
4   Serve sliced pork with sauce, apple and onions and, if you like, mashed or roasted potatoes.

prep & cook time 2 hours **serves** 6
nutritional count per serving 28.8g total fat (16.8g saturated fat); 2391kJ (572 cal); 14.7g carbohydrate; 55.1g protein; 3.8g fibre
notes Recipe is not suitable to freeze. Pork neck is a moist, tasty cut – it pot roasts really well. This is an easy way to cook: make sure the pan you use has a heavy base with a tight-fitting lid for even cooking. Granny Smith or Golden Delicious apples are best for this recipe.

chickpeas in spicy tomato sauce

¾ cup (150g) dried chickpeas
1 tablespoon olive oil
2 teaspoons cumin seeds
1 tablespoon ground
  coriander
¼ teaspoon cayenne pepper
1 medium brown onion (150g),
  chopped finely
2 cloves garlic, crushed
4cm piece fresh ginger (20g),
  grated
2 tablespoons tomato paste
800g can chopped tomatoes
1 cup (250ml) water
5 baby new potatoes (200g),
  quartered
10 baby carrots (200g),
  halved lengthways
½ cup coarsely chopped
  fresh coriander

1 Place chickpeas in medium bowl, cover with cold water; stand overnight, drain. Rinse under cold water; drain. Place chickpeas in medium saucepan of boiling water; return to the boil. Reduce heat; simmer, uncovered, about 1 hour or until tender; drain.

2 Heat oil in large saucepan; cook cumin, ground coriander and cayenne, stirring, until fragrant. Add onion, garlic and ginger; cook, stirring, until onion softens. Add tomato paste; cook, stirring, 2 minutes.

3 Add undrained tomatoes, the water, potato and chickpeas to pan; bring to the boil. Reduce heat; simmer, covered, about 30 minutes, stirring occasionally, until potato is tender and mixture is thickened.

4 Add carrot to pan; cook, uncovered, about 5 minutes or until carrot is tender. Remove from heat; stir in fresh coriander.

prep & cook time 2 hours (plus standing)
serves 4
nutritional count per serving 7.4g total fat
(1g saturated fat); 1062kJ (254 cal);
31.1g carbohydrate; 7.4g protein; 10.6g fibre
note Recipe, without the coriander, is suitable to freeze. Stir in coriander after reheating.

chicken and fig tagine

1 tablespoon olive oil
1kg chicken thigh fillets,
    chopped coarsely
1 medium red onion (170g),
    chopped finely
1 stalk celery (150g), trimmed,
    chopped coarsely
2 cloves garlic, crushed
1 teaspoon ground cumin
1 teaspoon ground coriander
1 teaspoon ground ginger
1 teaspoon ground cinnamon
1 teaspoon ground turmeric
2 cups (500ml) chicken stock
¾ cup (150g) dried figs,
    sliced thickly
1 medium red capsicum
    (200g), chopped coarsely
1 teaspoon finely grated
    lemon rind
¼ cup coarsely chopped
    fresh coriander
¼ cup (35g) coarsely chopped
    roasted unsalted pistachios

1 Heat oil in large saucepan; cook chicken, in batches, until browned.
2 Add onion, celery, garlic and spices to pan; cook, stirring, until onion softens.
3 Return chicken to pan; stir to coat in spice mixture. Add stock; bring to the boil. Reduce heat; simmer, covered, about 30 minutes or until chicken is almost cooked.
4 Add fig, capsicum and rind to pan; simmer, uncovered, about 15 minutes or until sauce thickens slightly.
5 Stir in fresh coriander; serve tagine sprinkled with nuts.

prep & cook time 1 hour 20 minutes
serves 4
nutritional count per serving 27.9g total fat (7g saturated fat); 2441kJ (584 cal); 27.2g carbohydrate; 52.6g protein; 8g fibre
note Recipe is not suitable to freeze.

in the oven

tomato-braised lamb shanks with creamy polenta

2 tablespoons olive oil

16 french-trimmed lamb shanks (4kg)

1 large red onion (300g), sliced thinly

1 clove garlic, crushed

2 tablespoons tomato paste

1 cup (250ml) dry red wine

2 cups (500ml) chicken stock

1 cup (250ml) water

400g can diced tomatoes

2 tablespoons coarsely chopped fresh rosemary

creamy polenta

3 cups (750ml) water

2 cups (500ml) milk

1 cup (250ml) chicken stock

1½ cups (250g) polenta

½ cup (40g) coarsely grated parmesan cheese

1 cup (250ml) cream

1 Preheat oven to 200°C/180°C fan-forced.

2 Heat half the oil in large flameproof baking dish on stove top; brown lamb, in batches.

3 Heat remaining oil in same dish; cook onion and garlic, stirring, until onion softens. Add paste; cook, stirring, 2 minutes. Add wine; bring to the boil. Boil, uncovered, until liquid reduces by about half.

4 Return lamb to dish with stock, the water, undrained tomatoes and rosemary; cover. Transfer dish to oven; cook, turning lamb occasionally, about 3 hours.

5 Make creamy polenta.

6 Divide polenta among serving plates; top with lamb, drizzle with pan juices.

creamy polenta Bring the water, milk and stock to the boil in medium saucepan; gradually stir in polenta. Cook, stirring, about 5 minutes or until polenta thickens slightly. Stir in cheese and cream.

prep & cook time 4 hours **serves** 8
nutritional count per serving 28g total fat (14.8g saturated fat); 2826kJ (676 cal); 30.3g carbohydrate; 69.1g protein; 2.3g fibre
notes You can halve the recipe to serve four. Recipe is suitable to freeze without the polenta.

lamb bretonne

You can use canned cannellini, navy, great northern or butter beans in this recipe.

1.5kg leg of lamb
1 clove garlic, sliced thinly
2 sprigs fresh rosemary
1 teaspoon sea salt flakes
½ teaspoon freshly cracked black pepper
20g butter
2 medium brown onions (300g), sliced thinly
3 cloves garlic, crushed
400g can diced tomatoes
410g can tomato puree
2 cups (500ml) beef stock
400g can white beans, rinsed, drained

1 Preheat oven to 180°C/160°C fan-forced.
2 Trim excess fat from lamb. Pierce lamb in several places with sharp knife; press sliced garlic and a little of the rosemary firmly into cuts. Rub salt and pepper over lamb.
3 Heat butter in large flameproof baking dish on stove top; cook onion and crushed garlic, stirring, until onion browns slightly. Stir in undrained tomatoes, puree, stock, beans and remaining rosemary; bring to the boil then remove from heat.
4 Place lamb, pierced-side down, on bean mixture; cover. Transfer dish to oven; cook 1 hour. Uncover, turn lamb carefully; cook, brushing occasionally with tomato mixture, about 1 hour or until lamb is cooked.

prep & cook time 2 hours 30 minutes **serves** 4
nutritional count per serving 19.9g total fat (9.5g saturated fat); 2324kJ (556 cal); 20.2g carbohydrate; 69.8g protein; 7.7g fibre
note Recipe is not suitable to freeze.

veal shin on mushroom ragoût

Ragoût, from a French word loosely meaning "appetite stimulator", is a luscious, slowly-cooked meat and vegetable stew.

40g butter
4 pieces veal osso buco (1.2kg)
2 cloves garlic, crushed
1 tablespoon fresh
   rosemary leaves
½ cup (125ml) port
1 cup (250ml) beef stock
mushroom ragoût
40g butter
2 cloves garlic, crushed
1 large flat mushroom (80g),
   sliced thickly
200g swiss brown
   mushrooms, trimmed
200g shiitake mushrooms,
   sliced thickly
1 medium red capsicum
   (200g), sliced thickly
1 medium green capsicum
   (200g), sliced thickly
½ cup (125ml) beef stock
2 tablespoons port

1 Preheat oven to 160°C/140°C fan-forced.
2 Melt butter in medium flameproof casserole dish on stove top; cook veal, uncovered, until browned both sides. Add garlic, rosemary, port and stock to pan; cover. Transfer dish to oven; cook 2¼ hours.
3 Make mushroom ragoût.
4 Divide veal and mushroom ragoût among serving dishes; serve with creamy polenta (see page 34), if you like.
mushroom ragoût Heat butter in large frying pan; cook garlic, mushrooms and capsicums, stirring, until vegetables are tender and browned lightly. Stir in stock and port; cook, covered, 30 minutes.

prep & cook time 2 hours 30 minutes
serves 4
nutritional count per serving 17.8g fat (11.1g saturated fat); 1735kJ (415 cal); 10.4g carbohydrate; 41.1g protein; 4.3g fibre
note Recipe is not suitable to freeze.

osso buco

6 large pieces veal osso buco
(1.8kg)
½ cup (75g) plain flour
40g butter
2 tablespoons olive oil
3 stalks celery (450g),
trimmed, chopped coarsely
6 drained anchovy fillets,
chopped coarsely
¾ cup (180ml) dry white wine
2 x 400g cans diced tomatoes
½ cup (125ml) chicken stock
5 cloves garlic, crushed
3 bay leaves
10 fresh thyme sprigs
gremolata
½ cup finely chopped fresh
flat-leaf parsley
2 cloves garlic, chopped finely
1 teaspoon finely grated
lemon rind

1 Preheat oven to 160°C/140°C fan-forced.
2 Coat veal in flour, shake off any excess.
Heat butter and oil in large frying pan on
stove top; cook veal, in batches, until
browned both sides. Transfer veal to large
ovenproof dish.
3 Cook celery and anchovy in same heated
pan, stirring, until celery softens. Add wine;
bring to the boil. Stir in undrained tomatoes,
stock, garlic, bay leaves and thyme; return
to the boil.
4 Pour tomato mixture over veal; cover.
Transfer dish to oven; cook about 1½ hours
or until veal starts to fall from the bone.
5 Make gremolata.
6 Serve osso buco sprinkled with gremolata.
Serve with creamy polenta (see page 34), if
you like.
gremolata Combine ingredients in small bowl.

prep & cook time 2 hours **serves** 6
nutritional count per serving 13.2g total fat
(4.8g saturated fat); 1626kJ (389 cal);
14.4g carbohydrate; 46.1g protein; 3.8g fibre
tips Osso buco can be made a day or two
ahead; keep, covered, in the refrigerator.
Reheat, covered tightly, in a moderate oven
for about 1 hour, or until heated through.
Make and use gremolata as close to serving
as possible. Stand the osso buco upright in
the ovenproof dish so the marrow doesn't
fall out (this is the best bit, so you don't want
anyone to miss out).

note Recipe, without the
gremolata, is suitable to
freeze for up to three
months. Make gremolata
close to the time of serving.

in the oven

braised beef cheeks in red wine

2 tablespoons olive oil
1.6kg beef cheeks, trimmed
1 medium brown onion (150g),
  chopped coarsely
1 medium carrot (120g),
  chopped coarsely
3 cups (750ml) dry red wine
¼ cup (60ml) red wine vinegar
2 x 400g cans whole
  tomatoes
¼ cup (55g) firmly packed
  brown sugar
2 sprigs fresh rosemary
6 black peppercorns
2 tablespoons fresh
  oregano leaves
1 large fennel bulb (550g),
  cut into thin wedges
400g spring onions, trimmed,
  halved
200g swiss brown mushrooms
cheesy polenta
2⅓ cups (580ml) water
2⅓ cups (580ml) milk
1 cup (170g) polenta
½ cup (40g) finely grated
  parmesan cheese
30g butter

1 Preheat oven to 160°C/140°C fan-forced.
2 Heat half the oil in large flameproof casserole dish on stove top; cook beef, in batches, until browned all over.
3 Heat remaining oil in same dish; cook brown onion and carrot, stirring, until onion softens. Return beef to dish with wine, vinegar, undrained tomatoes, sugar, rosemary, peppercorns, oregano and fennel; bring to the boil. Cover, transfer dish to oven; cook 2 hours.
4 Stir spring onion and mushrooms into dish; cook, uncovered, about 45 minutes or until beef is tender.
5 Meanwhile, make cheesy polenta; serve with beef.
cheesy polenta Combine the water and milk in large saucepan; bring to the boil. Gradually add polenta to liquid, stirring constantly. Reduce heat; simmer, stirring constantly, about 10 minutes or until polenta thickens. Stir in cheese and butter.

prep & cook time 3 hours 30 minutes
serves 4
nutritional count per serving 39.8g total fat (16.2g saturated fat); 4828 kJ (1155 cal); 67.1g carbohydrate; 100.8g protein; 10.3g fibre
note Recipe, without the polenta, is suitable to freeze.

braised veal shoulder with white beans

Ask your butcher to bone, roll and tie the veal shoulder for you.

¼ cup (60ml) olive oil
1.2kg boned veal shoulder, rolled, tied
2 medium brown onions (300g), sliced thickly
3 cloves garlic, crushed
½ cup (125ml) dry red wine
1 cinnamon stick
2 bay leaves
2 sprigs fresh rosemary
2 x 400g can diced tomatoes
½ cup (60g) seeded green olives
2 medium carrots (240g), chopped coarsely
½ cup (60g) frozen peas
400g can white beans, rinsed, drained

1 Preheat oven to 200°C/180°C fan-forced.
2 Heat 2 tablespoons of the oil in large flameproof baking dish on stove top; cook veal, turning frequently, until browned.
3 Heat remaining oil in same dish; cook onion and garlic, stirring, until onion softens. Add wine, cinnamon, bay leaves, rosemary, undrained tomatoes and olives; bring to the boil.
4 Return veal to dish; cover. Transfer to oven; cook, 30 minutes. Turn veal and stir tomato mixture. Add carrot; cook, covered, 30 minutes.
5 Remove veal from dish; cover to keep warm. Stir peas and beans into dish; cook, covered, 10 minutes.
6 Serve vegetables with sliced veal.

prep & cook time 1 hour 40 minutes **serves** 6
nutritional count per serving 14.7g total fat (2.8g saturated fat); 1697kJ (406 cal); 12.7g carbohydrate; 49.2g protein; 5.4g fibre
note Recipe is not suitable to freeze.

in the oven

italian braised pork

*Ask your butcher to roll and tie
the pork shoulder for you.*

2 tablespoons olive oil
1.5kg pork shoulder, rolled
　and tied
2 cloves garlic, crushed
1 medium brown onion (150g),
　chopped coarsely
½ small fennel bulb (100g),
　chopped coarsely
8 slices hot pancetta (120g),
　chopped coarsely
1 tablespoon tomato paste
½ cup (125ml) dry white wine
400g can whole tomatoes
1 cup (250ml) chicken stock
1 cup (250ml) water
2 sprigs fresh rosemary
2 large fennel bulbs (1kg),
　halved, sliced thickly
spice rub
1 teaspoon fennel seeds
2 teaspoons dried
　oregano leaves
½ teaspoon cayenne pepper
1 tablespoon cracked
　black pepper
1 tablespoon sea salt
2 teaspoons olive oil

1 Preheat oven to 180°C/160°C fan-forced.
2 Heat oil in large flameproof casserole dish on stove top; cook pork, uncovered, until browned all over.
3 Meanwhile, combine ingredients for spice rub in small bowl.
4 Remove pork from dish; discard all but 1 tablespoon of the oil in dish. Cook garlic, onion, chopped fennel and pancetta in same heated dish, stirring, until onion softens. Add paste; cook, stirring, 2 minutes.
5 Meanwhile, rub pork with spice rub.
6 Return pork to dish with wine, undrained tomatoes, stock, the water and rosemary; bring to the boil; cover. Transfer dish to oven; cook 1 hour.
7 Add sliced fennel to dish; cover. Return dish to oven; cook 1 hour. Remove pork from dish; discard pork rind. Cover pork to keep warm.
8 Meanwhile, cook braising liquid in dish, uncovered, over medium heat on stove top until thickened slightly. Serve sliced pork with sauce, and warm ciabatta bread, if desired.

prep & cook time 3 hours 15 minutes
serves 6
nutritional count per serving 32.8g total fat (10.7g saturated fat); 2525 kJ (604 cal); 7.5g carbohydrate; 66.5g protein; 4.6g fibre
note Recipe is not suitable to freeze.

vietnamese clay pot chicken

1kg chicken thigh fillets, chopped coarsely
½ cup (125ml) chicken stock
¼ cup (60ml) lime juice
2 tablespoons fish sauce
10cm stick fresh lemon grass (20g), chopped finely
1cm piece fresh ginger (5g), grated
1 clove garlic, crushed
150g small oyster mushrooms
450g baby buk choy, chopped coarsely
4 green onions, sliced diagonally
1 fresh small red thai chilli, sliced thinly
¼ cup loosely packed fresh coriander leaves
¼ cup loosely packed fresh vietnamese mint leaves

1 Preheat oven to 180°C/160°C fan-forced.
2 Combine chicken, stock, juice, sauce, lemon grass, ginger and garlic in 2-litre (8-cup) clay pot or ovenproof dish. Cook, covered, 30 minutes. Add mushrooms and buk choy to dish; cover. Return dish to oven; cook a further 30 minutes or until chicken is cooked through. Serve chicken mixture topped with remaining ingredients.

prep & cook time 1 hour 15 minutes **serves** 4
nutritional count per serving 18.6g total fat (5.6g saturated fat); 1626kJ (389 cal); 3.2g carbohydrate; 50.6g protein; 4g fibre
tips Recipe is not suitable to freeze. Before using a clay pot, soak it in water for about 15 minutes; this releases steam during the cooking process, which helps create a tender, flavourful dish.

roasts

port and balsamic slow-roasted lamb

2.5kg leg of lamb
¼ cup (30g) sea salt flakes
20g butter
1 tablespoon olive oil
⅓ cup (80ml) dry red wine
⅓ cup (80ml) balsamic vinegar
⅓ cup (80ml) port
¼ cup (60ml) beef stock
8 cloves garlic, crushed
8 medium egg tomatoes (600g), halved lengthways

1 Preheat oven to 120°C/100°C fan-forced.
2 Bring large saucepan of water to the boil; add lamb, simmer 15 minutes. Drain; pat lamb dry. Pierce lamb all over with sharp knife; press salt into cuts.
3 Heat butter and oil in large flameproof dish; cook lamb, turning, until browned all over. Add wine, vinegar, port, stock and garlic to dish; cover. Transfer dish to oven; roast lamb 4½ hours.
4 Add tomatoes, cut-side up, to dish with lamb; roast, uncovered, a further 2 hours, basting occasionally.
5 Remove lamb and tomatoes from dish. Boil pan juices until reduced by half; serve with lamb.

prep & cook time 7 hours 20 minutes serves 6
nutritional count per serving 22.7g total fat (9.7g saturated fat); 2186kJ (52 cal); 4.5g carbohydrate; 69.6g protein; 2.1g fibre
note Recipe is not suitable to freeze.

lamb shanks in five-spice, tamarind and ginger

2 teaspoons five-spice powder
1 teaspoon dried chilli flakes
1 cinnamon stick
2 star anise
¼ cup (60ml) soy sauce
½ cup (125ml) chinese
  cooking wine
2 tablespoons tamarind
  concentrate
2 tablespoons brown sugar
8cm piece fresh ginger (40g),
  grated
2 cloves garlic, chopped
  coarsely
1¼ cups (310ml) water
8 french-trimmed
  lamb shanks (2kg)
150g sugar snap peas,
  trimmed
500g choy sum, chopped
  into 10cm lengths

1 Preheat oven to 180°C/160°C fan-forced.
2 Dry-fry five-spice, chilli, cinnamon and star anise in small frying pan, stirring, until fragrant. Combine spices with sauce, cooking wine, tamarind, sugar, ginger, garlic and the water in medium jug.
3 Place lamb, in single layer, in large shallow baking dish; drizzle with spice mixture. Roast, uncovered, in oven, turning lamb occasionally, about 2 hours or until meat is almost falling off the bone. Remove lamb from dish; cover to keep warm. Skim excess fat from pan juices; strain juices into small saucepan, discard solids.
4 Meanwhile, boil, steam or microwave peas and choy sum, separately, until tender; drain.
5 Divide vegetables and lamb among serving plates; serve drizzled with reheated pan juices.

prep & cook time 2 hours 30 minutes
serves 4
nutritional count per serving 25g total fat (11.3g saturated fat); 2370kJ (567 cal); 13.1g carbohydrate; 61.6g protein; 6.5g fibre
note Recipe, without the vegetables, is suitable to freeze. Cook vegetables close to serving time.

slow-roasted honey and soy pork neck

1 tablespoon peanut oil
1kg piece pork neck
1 large brown onion (200g),
  sliced thinly
2 cloves garlic, sliced thinly
4cm piece fresh ginger (20g),
  sliced thinly
1 cinnamon stick
2 star anise
½ cup (125ml) salt-reduced
  soy sauce
½ cup (125ml) chinese
  cooking wine
¼ cup (90g) honey
1 cup (250ml) water
450g baby buk choy, trimmed,
  leaves separated

1 Preheat oven to 160°C/140°C fan-forced.
2 Heat oil in large flameproof casserole dish; cook pork, turning occasionally, until browned. Remove from dish. Add onion, garlic and ginger to same heated dish; cook, stirring, until onion softens. Remove from heat.
3 Stir cinnamon, star anise, sauce, cooking wine, honey and the water into onion mixture in dish. Return pork to dish, turning to coat in spice mixture.
4 Cover dish; transfer to oven. Cook 1 hour. Uncover; cook about 1 hour or until sauce thickens slightly. Remove pork from dish. Cover pork; stand 10 minutes before slicing.
5 Add buk choy to dish; cook, stirring, over medium heat on stove top, about 5 minutes or until just tender. Serve pork with buk choy and sauce.

prep & cook time 2 hours 35 minutes
serves 4
nutritional count per serving 30.6g total fat (9.8g saturated fat); 2621kJ (627 cal); 5.9g carbohydrate; 76.4g protein; 2.5g fibre
note Recipe is not suitable to freeze.

greek roast lamb with skordalia and lemon-scented potatoes

2kg leg of lamb
2 cloves garlic, crushed
½ cup (125ml) lemon juice
2 tablespoons olive oil
1 tablespoon fresh
 oregano leaves
1 teaspoon fresh
 lemon thyme leaves
5 large potatoes (1.5kg), cut
 into 3cm pieces
2 tablespoons olive oil, extra
1 tablespoon finely grated
 lemon rind
2 tablespoons lemon juice
1 teaspoon fresh
 lemon thyme leaves
skordalia
1 medium potato (200g),
 quartered
3 cloves garlic, quartered
1 tablespoon lemon juice
1 tablespoon white wine
 vinegar
2 tablespoons water
⅓ cup (80ml) olive oil
1 tablespoon warm water

1 Combine lamb with garlic, juice, oil, oregano and thyme in large bowl. Cover; refrigerate 3 hours or overnight.
2 Preheat oven to 160°C/140°C fan-forced.
3 Place lamb in large baking dish; roast, uncovered, 4 hours.
4 Make skordalia.
5 Toss potato in large bowl with combined remaining ingredients; place, in single layer, on oven tray. Roast potato, uncovered, for last 30 minutes of lamb cooking time.
6 Remove lamb from oven; cover.
7 Increase oven temperature to 220°C/200°C fan-forced; roast potatoes a further 20 minutes or until crisp and tender. Serve potatoes and lamb with skordalia; sprinkle with extra fresh lemon thyme leaves, if you like.

skordalia Boil, steam or microwave potato until tender; drain. Push through food mill or fine sieve into large bowl; cool 10 minutes. Place garlic, juice, vinegar and the water in bowl with potato; stir until well combined. Place potato mixture in blender; with motor operating, gradually add oil in a thin, steady stream, blending only until skordalia thickens (do not overmix). Stir in the water.

prep & cook time 4 hours 30 minutes (plus refrigeration) **serves** 4
nutritional count per serving 57g total fat (14g saturated fat); 4556kJ (1090 cal); 51.5g carbohydrate; 91.2g protein; 6.7g fibre

note Recipe is not suitable to freeze.

crispy-skinned roast chicken with tomato-braised beans

2kg whole chicken
1 medium lemon (140g),
    quartered
6 sprigs fresh thyme
6 cloves garlic, unpeeled
60g butter, softened
2 tablespoons lemon juice
2 cloves garlic, crushed
2 teaspoons finely chopped
    fresh thyme
1 cup (250ml) water
1 tablespoon olive oil
1 medium brown onion (150g),
    chopped coarsely
1kg green beans, trimmed
4 medium tomatoes (600g),
    chopped coarsely

1 Preheat oven to 200°C/180°C fan-forced.
2 Rinse chicken under cold water; pat dry inside and out with absorbent paper. Tuck wing tips under chicken. Fill cavity with lemon, thyme sprigs and unpeeled garlic, fold skin over to enclose filling; secure with toothpicks. Tie legs together with kitchen string.
3 Combine butter, juice, crushed garlic and chopped thyme in small bowl; rub butter mixture all over chicken.
4 Place chicken on oiled rack in large baking dish; pour the water into dish. Roast about 2 hours, basting occasionally with pan juices.
5 Meanwhile, heat oil in large saucepan; cook onion, stirring, until soft. Add beans and tomato; cook, covered, over medium heat, stirring occasionally, about 20 minutes or until vegetables soften slightly.
6 Serve chicken with bean and tomato mixture, and roast potatoes, if you like.

prep & cook time 2 hours 40 minutes
serves 6
nutritional count per serving 33.5g total fat (12.7g saturated fat); 2123kJ (508 cal); 8.3g carbohydrate; 40.3g protein; 7.3g fibre
note Recipe is not suitable to freeze.

glossary

artichokes, jerusalem
neither from Jerusalem nor an artichoke, this crunchy tuber tastes a bit like a fresh water chestnut and is related to the sunflower family.

beans
borlotti also known as roman beans or pink beans, are available fresh or dried. They are interchangeable with pinto beans because of the similarity in appearance – both are pale pink or beige with dark red streaks.
cannellini see beans, white.
white many varieties of white beans are available canned, among them great northern, navy, cannellini, butter and haricot beans, all of which can be substituted for each other.

beef
chuck steak taken from the shoulder; isn't as tender as other cuts, so is best if slow-roasted or braised.
gravy (beef shin) cut from the lower shin; commonly used in stews and braises. Also known as a shank.
buk choy also known as bok choy, pak choi, chinese white cabbage or chinese chard; has a fresh, mild mustard taste. Baby buk choy, also known as pak kat farang or shanghai bok choy, is smaller and more tender.
butter use salted or unsalted (sweet) butter; 125g is equal to one stick of butter.

capsicum also known as bell pepper or, simply, pepper. They come in many colours; red, yellow, orange, green and purple-black. Discard seeds and membranes before use.

chillies generally the smaller the chilli, the hotter it is. Use rubber gloves when seeding and chopping fresh chillies to prevent burning your skin. Removing membranes and seeds lessens the heat level.
flakes deep-red, dehydrated chilli slices and whole seeds.
long red available fresh and dried; a generic term used for any moderately hot, long, thin chilli (about 6-8cm long).
red thai small, medium hot, and bright red in colour.

chinese cooking wine also known as chinese rice wine or hao hsing; made from fermented rice, wheat, sugar and salt with a 13.5 per cent alcohol content. Inexpensive and found in Asian food shops; if you can't find it, replace with mirin or sherry.

chorizo a sausage of Spanish origin, made of coarsely ground pork and seasoned with garlic and chillies.

choy sum also known as pakaukeo or flowering cabbage, a member of the buk choy family; easy to identify with its long stems, light green leaves and yellow flowers. Is eaten, stems and all.

coriander also known as pak chee, cilantro or chinese parsley; bright-green leafy herb with a pungent flavour. The stems and roots are also used; wash well before using. Coriander seeds are also available but are no substitute for fresh coriander, as the taste is very different.

fish fillets, firm white any boneless firm white fish fillet. Blue eye, bream, swordfish, ling, whiting or sea perch are all good choices. Check for any small pieces of bone and use tweezers to remove them.

five-spice powder a mix of ground cinnamon, star anise, cloves, sichuan pepper and fennel seeds. Also known as chinese five-spice.

flour, plain an all-purpose flour made from wheat.

galangal a rhizome with a hot ginger-citrusy flavour; used similarly to ginger. Substitute with fresh ginger if unavailable.

ginger, fresh also known as green or root ginger; the thick root of a tropical plant.
ground also known as powdered ginger; cannot be substituted for fresh ginger.

kaffir lime leaves also known as bai magrood; looks like two glossy dark green leaves joined end to end, forming a rounded hourglass shape. A strip of fresh lime peel may be substituted for each kaffir lime leaf.

kitchen string made of a natural product such as cotton or hemp so that it neither affects the flavour of the food it's tied around nor melts when heated.

lemon grass a tall, clumping, lemon-smelling and -tasting, sharp-edged grass; the white lower part of the stem is used, finely chopped, in cooking.

onions

green also known as scallion or, incorrectly, shallot; an immature onion picked before the bulb has formed, having a long, bright-green edible stalk.

red also known as spanish, red spanish or bermuda onion; a sweet-flavoured, large, purple-red onion.

shallots also called french shallots, golden shallots or eschalots; brown-skinned, small, elongated members of the onion family.

spring onions with small white bulbs and long narrow green-leafed tops.

oregano also known as wild marjoram; has a woody stalk with clumps of tiny, dark green leaves that have a pungent, peppery flavour. Available fresh or dried.

pancetta, hot an Italian style of bacon; is lean pork belly that is salted and cured (but not smoked) then spiced and rolled into a fat, sausage-like loaf. It is available from most delicatessens.

parsley, flat-leaf also known as continental parsley or italian parsley.

patty-pan squash also known as crookneck or custard marrow pumpkins; a round, slightly flat summer squash being yellow to pale-green in colour and having a scalloped edge.

pearl barley has had the husk removed then been hulled and polished so only the "pearl" of the original grain remains, much the same as white rice.

polenta also known as cornmeal; a flour-like cereal made of dried corn (maize) sold ground in different textures; also the name of the dish made from it.

potatoes, baby new also known as chats.

prawns also known as shrimp.

risoni pasta is a small rice-shaped pasta, very similar to orzo, and is often used as the pasta of choice when making soup.

sauces

fish also called nam pla or nuoc nam; made from pulverised salted fermented fish, most often anchovies. Has a pungent smell and strong taste, so use according to your taste.

soy made from fermented soya beans. Several variations are available in most supermarkets and Asian food stores.

spinach also known as english spinach and, incorrectly, silver beet.

star anise dried star-shaped pod having an astringent aniseed flavour.

sugar, brown an extremely soft, finely granulated sugar retaining molasses for its colour and flavour.

tamarind concentrate (or paste) the commercial result of the distillation of tamarind juice into a condensed, compacted paste. Thick and purple-black, it is ready-to-use, with no soaking or straining required; can be diluted with water according to taste.

vietnamese mint not a mint at all, but a pungent and peppery narrow-leafed member of the buckwheat family; also known as laksa leaf and cambodian mint.

vinegar

balsamic made from the juice of Trebbiano grapes; it is a deep rich brown colour with a sweet and sour flavour. Pungency depends on how long it's been aged. Quality can be determined up to a point by price; use the most expensive sparingly.

red wine based on fermented red wine.

white wine made from a blend of white wines.

zucchini also known as courgette; a member of the squash family.

conversion chart

MEASURES

One Australian metric measuring cup holds approximately 250ml, one Australian metric tablespoon holds 20ml, one Australian metric teaspoon holds 5ml.

The difference between one country's measuring cups and another's is within a 2- or 3-teaspoon variance, and will not affect your cooking results. North America, New Zealand and the United Kingdom use a 15ml tablespoon. All cup and spoon measurements are level. The most accurate way of measuring dry ingredients is to weigh them. When measuring liquids, use a clear glass or plastic jug with metric markings.

We use large eggs with an average weight of 60g.

DRY MEASURES

METRIC	IMPERIAL
15g	½oz
30g	1oz
60g	2oz
90g	3oz
125g	4oz (¼lb)
155g	5oz
185g	6oz
220g	7oz
250g	8oz (½lb)
280g	9oz
315g	10oz
345g	11oz
375g	12oz (¾lb)
410g	13oz
440g	14oz
470g	15oz
500g	16oz (1lb)
750g	24oz (1½lb)
1kg	32oz (2lb)

LIQUID MEASURES

METRIC	IMPERIAL
30ml	1 fluid oz
60ml	2 fluid oz
100ml	3 fluid oz
125ml	4 fluid oz
150ml	5 fluid oz (¼ pint/1 gill)
190ml	6 fluid oz
250ml	8 fluid oz
300ml	10 fluid oz (½ pint)
500ml	16 fluid oz
600ml	20 fluid oz (1 pint)
1000ml (1 litre)	1¾ pints

LENGTH MEASURES

METRIC	IMPERIAL
3mm	⅛in
6mm	¼in
1cm	½in
2cm	¾in
2.5cm	1in
5cm	2in
6cm	2½in
8cm	3in
10cm	4in
13cm	5in
15cm	6in
18cm	7in
20cm	8in
23cm	9in
25cm	10in
28cm	11in
30cm	12in (1ft)

OVEN TEMPERATURES

These oven temperatures are only a guide for conventional ovens. For fan-forced ovens, check the manufacturer's manual.

	°C (CELSIUS)	°F (FAHRENHEIT)	GAS MARK
Very slow	120	250	½
Slow	150	275-300	1-2
Moderately slow	160	325	3
Moderate	180	350-375	4-5
Moderately hot	200	400	6
Hot	220	425-450	7-8
Very hot	240	475	9

index

ACP BOOKS
General manager Christine Whiston
Editor-in-chief Susan Tomnay
Creative director Hieu Chi Nguyen
Art director + designer Hannah Blackmore
Senior editor Wendy Bryant
Food writer Xanthe Roberts
Food director Pamela Clark
Test Kitchen manager + nutritional information Belinda Farlow
Sales & rights director Brian Cearnes
Marketing manager Bridget Cody
Senior business analyst Rebecca Varela
Circulation manager Jarna Mclean
Operations manager David Scotto
Production manager Victoria Jefferys

ACP Books are published by ACP Magazines
a division of PBL Media Pty Limited
PBL Media, Chief Executive officer Ian Law
Publishing & sales director, Women's lifestyle Lynette Phillips
Group editorial director, Women's lifestyle Pat Ingram
Marketing director, Women's lifestyle Matthew Dominello
Commercial manager, Women's lifestyle Seymour Cohen
Research Director, Women's lifestyle Justin Stone

Produced by ACP Books, Sydney.

Published by ACP Books, a division of ACP Magazines Ltd, 54 Park St, Sydney; GPO Box 4088, Sydney, NSW 2001.
phone (02) 9282 8618; fax (02) 9267 9438. acpbooks@acpmagazines.com.au; www.acpbooks.com.au

Printed by Dai Nippon in Korea.

Australia Distributed by Network Services, phone +61 2 9282 8777; fax +61 2 9264 3278;
networkweb@networkservicescompany.com.au
United Kingdom Distributed by Australian Consolidated Press (UK), phone (01604) 642 200;
fax (01604) 642 300; books@acpuk.com
New Zealand Distributed by Netlink Distribution Company, phone (9) 366 9966; ask@ndc.co.nz
South Africa Distributed by PSD Promotions, phone (27 11) 392 6065/6/7;
fax (27 11) 392 6079/80; orders@psdprom.co.za
Canada Distributed by Publishers Group Canada
phone (800) 663 5714; fax (800) 565 3770; service@raincoast.com
Title: Slow cooked / food director Pamela Clark.
ISBN: 978 186396 856 0 (pbk.)
Subjects: Electric cookery, Slow.
Other Authors/Contributors: Clark, Pamela.
Dewey Number: 641.5884
© ACP Magazines Ltd 2009
ABN 18 053 273 546

Cover Chickpeas in spicy tomato sauce, page 30
Photographer Ian Wallace
Stylist Louise Pickford
Food preparation Kellie-Marie Thomas

Send recipe enquiries to:
recipeenquiries@acpmagazines.com.au